DISCARD

It's Summer!

By Linda Glaser

Illustrated by Susan Swan

The Millbrook Press   Brookfield, Connecticut

To Chris DeGoyler and Susan Marinsky Cramer who opened my world to
the incomparable joy of backpacking, many long summers ago on the Finger
Lakes Trail. And special thanks to Billie Anderson and Ruth Worley for
their expertise and enthusiasm with all four *Celebrate the Seasons* books.
LG

For Terry Rasberry, with love and admiration.
SS

Library of Congress Cataloging-in-Publication Data
It's summer! / by Linda Glaser ; illustrated by Susan Swan.
p. cm. — (Celebrate the seasons!)
Summary: A child observes the coming of summer and its effects on the weather,
animals, and plants. Includes suggestions for summertime activities to enjoy alone or with a parent.
ISBN 0-7613-1757-0 (lib. bdg.) — ISBN 0-7613-1735-X (pbk.)
[1. Summer—Fiction.] 1. Swan, Susan, ill. II. Series.
PZ7 .I915 2003   [E]—dc21   2001008631
Copyright © 2003 by Linda Glaser
Illustrations copyright © 2003 by Susan Swan

Published by The Millbrook Press, Inc.
2 Old New Milford Road
Brookfield, Connecticut 06804
www.millbrookpress.com

Manufactured in USA
5 4 3 2 1   (lib. bdg.)
5 4 3 2 1   (pbk.)

It's
Summer!

I flop down in the grass and watch clouds float by.
They glide and swirl across the sky.

Dragonflies zip here and there.

Butterflies flit around in the warm summer air.

I watch ants scurry to a small anthill.
I find a spider in its web sitting very still.
A caterpillar inches along a leaf. And here's
a little ladybug—landed right on me!

A baby robin flaps its wings and flies a short
way. Its mother still feeds it. But soon it will
learn to feed itself. Then it will fly away.

It's summer!
We make little mud houses
and tiny trees out of dirt and water
and sticks and leaves.
Cool mud sucks at our toes in
such a squishy way. It's so warm
and sunny we could play
outside all day.

Some days we get all hot and sweaty.
Some days we go to the beach or the pool.
We pull on our swimsuits and smear on sunscreen.
Then we splash around and get nice and cool.

We pack plenty of summer fruits to eat!
Peaches, melons, cherries, berries—
all juicy and sweet.

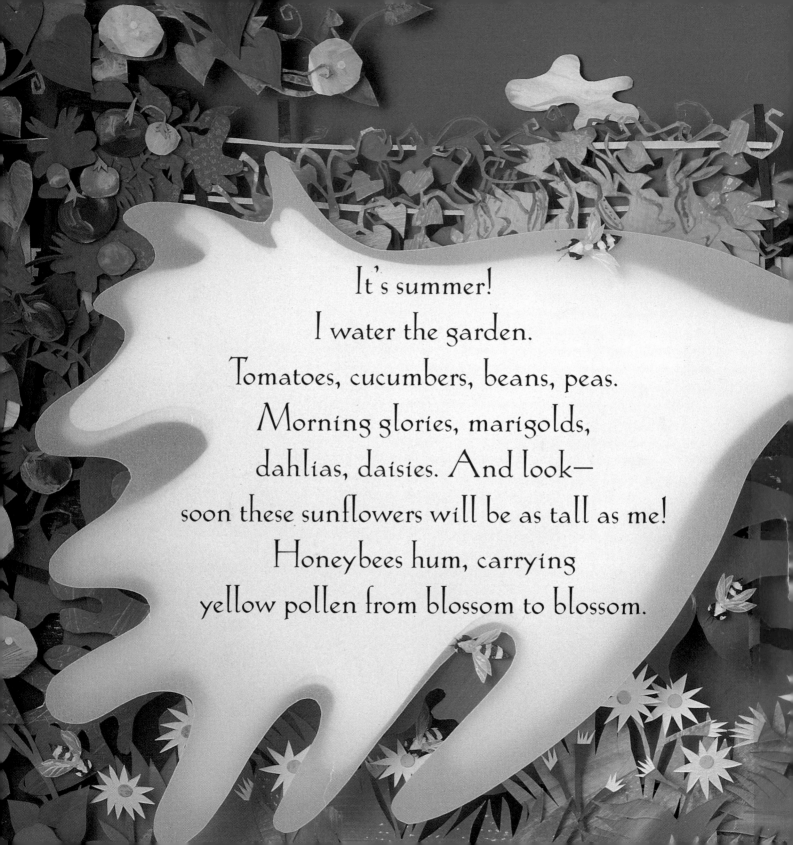

It's summer!
I water the garden.
Tomatoes, cucumbers, beans, peas.
Morning glories, marigolds,
dahlias, daisies. And look—
soon these sunflowers will be as tall as me!
Honeybees hum, carrying
yellow pollen from blossom to blossom.

There's an itchy,
whiny
buzzing sound. I swish my arms
and slap around every which way.
But OUCH!
That mosquito gets me anyway.

One day, the sky turns dark and cloudy.
Wind whips and whistles through the trees.

BOOM, BOOM, BOOM!
Thunder crashes! Lightning flashes! We dash inside.
SPLISH, SPLISH, SPLASH.
It's a thunderstorm!

After the rain,
the air smells fresh and clean.
We float leaves and twigs
down tiny streams.
And look way up high!
A rainbow curves
across the sky.

It's summer!
After dinner, it's still so light,
it doesn't even look like night.
As it grows dark,
the bats come out.
They zip and dart
and swoop about.

In the black of night,

we spot tiny winks of yellow light.

Fireflies! Fireflies! Blinking here and there,

like sparks of magic in the air.

I catch one in a jar and watch it glow,

then lift off the lid and let it go.

One day a yellow leaf floats down.
And there's another

falling to the ground.

A sudden crispness stirs the air.
Soon, very soon, fall will be here.
But right now it's still summer.

Everything's growing—the birds, the bugs,
the animals, the trees . . . the fruits,
the flowers, the grass, the weeds.
And look—now my sunflowers
are way taller than me.

We run around and explore and play.
Hooray! It's summer! Hooray!

Nature Activities to Do When It's Summer

Make daisy or clover chains.
Slit a hole in the stem of a clover
flower with your fingernail.
Then slip another clover stem
through it. Slit that stem, and so on.

Hunt for four-leaf clovers. Some people think
it's good luck to find one.

Watch out for poison ivy—it has three shiny
leaves. If you see it, don't touch it.

Go berry picking with a grown-up.
Pick raspberries or blueberries or strawberries.
Eat only berries that a grown-up says are safe to eat.

Watch insects—ants, spiders, caterpillars, and sow bugs are all easy to
find and interesting to watch. Try viewing them under a magnifying glass.

Find a caterpillar. Put it in a lidded jar with holes on top. Give it a fresh supply
of the type of leaf you found it on. That's its food. Over time, watch it form a
chrysalis and emerge as a butterfly. Then let it go.

Grow your own garden with a grown-up. If you have a yard, ask for a small sunny spo
to plant your choice of flowers or vegetables. If you don't have a yard, you can still grow
window garden in a sunny window or on a porch or terrace. Many flowers do well in a
sunny spot outside in a pot. Strawberries, lettuce, radishes, peas, bush beans, and tomatoe
can grow in pots. Use big pots for big plants like tomatoes.

Start a compost pile in the backyard. An adult can construct a simple compost bin by
forming chicken wire into a cylinder. Add grass clippings and leftover vegetables and
fruits to the pile. To speed up the composting, an adult can toss it with a pitchfork
every week or so. If it's dry, sprinkle it with some water. Soon,
the leftovers turn into rich brown compost for the garden.

Take a night outing with a grown-up. See if you
discover any night animals. Watch the stars. See
which constellations you can identify. In
August, watch the meteor showers.

Make a flower arrangement. Ask an adult which flowers you can pick. Put them in a vase filled with water. Set them on the kitchen table to enjoy.

Press flowers. Ask an adult which flowers you can pick. Arrange them carefully inside an old telephone book. Stack some other books on top. In a few weeks, the flowers will be pressed and ready to glue carefully on a piece of paper.

Feed the birds. Put out birdseed. Keep track of all the birds that come.

Examine small mosses, lichens, and flowers under a magnifying glass.

Plant a butterfly garden with flowering plants that attract butterflies. Butterflies especially like red, orange, yellow, and purple flowers—in large, bright masses of color.

Take a rain walk. Ask a grown-up to take you outside during a light, warm summer rain. Notice the smells and the sounds. Look for a rainbow if the sun comes out right after the rain.

Use twigs, rocks, dirt, leaves, and weeds to create a tiny village or forest home.

Watch buds form and flowers bloom. Watch as the flowers turn into seeds.

About the Author and Illustrator

Linda Glaser is the author of many successful nonfiction picture books on natural history subjects. Her books SPECTACULAR SPIDERS, COMPOST!, WONDERFUL WORMS, and OUR BIG HOME: AN EARTH POEM were all named Outstanding Science Trade Books for Children by the Children's Book Council/National Science Teachers Association, and OUR BIG HOME is a Reading Rainbow selection. In addition to teaching and writing, she conducts writing workshops for schoolchildren and for adults. She lives in Minnesota.

For IT'S SUMMER, Susan Swan created three-dimensional cut-paper artwork. First she selected her papers and then hand painted them to get the colors and textures she needed to achieve the palette of summer. She then layered the papers to accomplish the dramatic sense of depth that gives life to each piece of art. Finally, Susan's husband, Terry, photographed the finished artwork with lighting that accents the shadows of the paper. Susan and her husband are, professionally, Swan & Rasberry Studios, and they live in Texas.